# BONSAI

In the space you can encompass with your arms, the art of bonsai encapsulates nature. A single bonsai can convey a scene of a lone pine hanging from a precipice or a dense grove of maples. Whether gracing the alcove of a traditional tearoom, standing at the center of a grand hall, or resting on the balcony of a crowded apartment building, a bonsai expresses the mystery of life, a sense of beauty, and the ability to endure and prevail.

Bonsai, literally "planted in a tray," are common, potted trees—pine, bamboo, and Japanese plum are among the favorites—ranging in height from two inches to three feet. Constant pruning, repotting, and controlling the amounts of sun, water, and nutrients they receive keep the trees small. As such, bonsai exemplify the Japanese aesthetic belief tha[...] only after [...] "naturaln[...] manipulat[...]

The beauty of a bonsai is judged by its entire form and style, not just its flowers or foliage. Hence, a cultivator takes special care in the spacing of the branches and their arrangement, the angle of elevation, the contrast between delicate buds and a coarse, aged trunk, and the harmony between the plant and the pot. Over time, several distinct styles have emerged: straight trunk, cascading, slanting, curved trunk, twin trunk, patterned, clumped, and forest. Yet ultimately, like their counterparts in nature, no bonsai is like any other; each is a unique manifestation of nature and the artist's individual aesthetic sensibility.

Bonsai originally came to Japan from China with the introduction of Zen Buddhism in the late Kamakura period (1185-1333). Monks and noblemen first grew them to express Zen Buddhist sentiments such as the belief that "the infinitesimal is identical with the enormous." By the late Edo period (1600-1868), the art of bonsai had become, and remains today, a popular hobby enjoyed by all people. Growing bonsai, as indicated by the precept "it takes three years to master the art of watering," requires time and patience. Mastering the basics takes five to ten years. For many people, the care even a single bonsai requires draws them away from their hectic, modern lives and offers a chance to nurture and reaffirm a belief in the ever-renewing life force. If properly cared for, a bonsai can live hundreds of years. Bonsai are prized not only for their inherent beauty but as a legacy from previous generations and symbols of timelessness and continuity.

# Notes on the Illustrations

### 1. *Kuromatsu* (Japanese black pine), Cascade, 120 years, 45 inches
This rare cascade-style Japanese black pine draws the awed attention of viewers with its amazing balancing act. The lower branch billows in elegant, green tiers.

### 2. *Hime-mosochiku* (Bamboo), Natural, 5 years, 29 inches
On a piece of moss-covered rock stands an island of slender bamboo—a type of tree only recently used for bonsai. With a slight breeze, the fronds of the leaves rustle and sway. Every morning before the dew dries, a strip of skin from each bamboo is removed to keep the bamboo separated and thin.

### 3. *Kan-kobai* (Japanese apricot), Curved trunk, 70 years, 23 inches
The twisted and flattened trunk curves with stoic grace to display the bonsai's deep pink blossoms, which begin to flower while still in the midst of winter's cold.

### 4. *Yabai* (Japanese apricot), Curved trunk, 120 years, 21 inches
In their full glory, the apricot blossoms cover the tree—a feat difficult to achieve, as the Japanese apricot does not readily bud. The rugged trunk with its strong curve harmonizes with the delicacy of the blossoms.

### 5. *Obai* (Winter jasmine), Curved trunk, 90 years, 15 inches
While the gnarled and knotted trunk merits respect on its own terms, its artistry becomes all the more remarkable when one considers that the winter jasmine is a climbing tree, highly resistant to forming a trunk. In early spring, sharp yellow blossoms bud and bloom above the thick moss and exposed roots.

### 6. *Ume* (Japanese apricot), Curved trunk, 120 years, 26 inches

The age-marked trunk twists and careens in a sweeping right curve, creating a sense of elegant movement. The delicately ramified lower branches, with their small, precious flowers, exemplify features that make this the favored variety of Japanese apricot for bonsai.

### 7. *Hinoki* (Japanese cypress), Straight trunk, 150 years, 45 inches

Said to be found on the upper reaches of the Isuzu River above the Ise Grand Shrine, this straight-trunked bonsai's classic proportions, dense foliage, and delicate outer branches convey a sense of purity and tranquillity. The late Emperor received this bonsai from a prime minister to mark the inception of a new cabinet and the Emperor's birthday.

### 8. *Ezomatsu* (Yezo spruce), Root-linked, 200 years, 24 inches

Carefully angled so that no tree overwhelms another, this bonsai is a miniature forest of yezo spruce. Smaller trunks heighten the stature of greater trunks. Exposed, ridged roots give texture to the forest floor.

### 9. *Boke* (Flowering quince), Clump, 100 years, 12 inches

Its varicolored blossoms and beauty make the flowering quince popular among bonsai cultivators. The energetic twisting and turning of the branches belies the tree's age.

### 10. *Hikan-zakura* (Japanese cherry), Curved trunk, 80 years, 28 inches

Beginning with a twist at its base, soft and sinuous curves extend to even the tiniest branches of this coquettish cherry tree. The pale green container tastefully sets off the salmon pink, winter blossoms.

### 11. *Shio* (Azalea), Natural, 29 inches

Bright pink blossoms epitomize youth and vivacity, while the larger trunk lends a sense of somber weight and age. Subtle angling of the branches sets the bonsai slightly out of symmetry.

### 12. *Takasago* (Azalea), Natural, 33 inches

The charming, soft flower of the azalea almost hides the short, stout trunk. The square pot subtly counterbalances the round-edged, triangular shape of the bonsai.

### 13. *Yamatsutsuji* (Torch azalea), Clump, 100 years, 22 inches

Careful manicure and attention to proportion only heightens the natural freshness of this bonsai. Exposed roots grip the earth around the trunk. In the early summer, sweet, pink buds cover the tips of the delicate branches.

### 14. *Kinsai* (Azalea), Natural, 23 inches

The roots clench the earth in full circle around the trunk, while the flowers seem to crane upward toward the skies. With each ascending group, the branch formations become increasingly compact and dense. The dark blue pot draws out the luminous colors of the flowers and buds.

### 15. *Goyomatsu* (Japanese white pine), Curved trunk, 500 years, 29 inches

The third Tokugawa shogun, Iemitsu (1604-1651), assigned three attendants to care for this prized bonsai. The *ichi-no-eda*, or first main branch, which folds into itself, seems to manifest the mysterious life force which has protected this bonsai for half a millennium.

### 16. *Tosho* (Needle juniper), Straight trunk, 550 years, 35 inches

This venerable bonsai stands with regal magnificence, as if unfazed by its relative neglect till 1950 and its subsequent damage from a typhoon. Since then, this needle juniper has received the care and reverent admiration of the bonsai world.

### 17. *Kaede* (Japanese maple), Twin trunk, 80 years, 34 inches

Austere, weathered bark characterizes this variety of Japanese maple. The balance achieved by the tender leaf buds and delicate, smaller branches counterpointing the trunk is only possible with this variety of Japanese maple.

### 18. *Momiji* (Japanese maple), Curved trunk, 50 years, 19 inches

When this Japanese maple begins budding, crimson spreads like fire over the tree, prompting the tribute "king of leaves." A single branch of this bonsai stretches out to the left of the pale green container, suggesting the flow of a gentle stream below.

### 19. Keyaki (Japanese zelkova), Broom, 55 years, 28 inches

Though this tree originally grew in a garden and had branches over three yards long, expert tending and complex, deliberate control of its growth transformed it into a beautiful bonsai—stark in the winter, lush and green in the spring and summer, and red-, orange-, and yellow-hued in the fall.

### 20. Keyaki (Japanese zelkova), Group planting, 25 years, 26 inches

With its outer trees so markedly smaller and thinner than the central ones, this group bonsai projects the feeling of a magical wonderland. A continuing process of adopting and rejecting underlies the beauty of this work.

### 21. Kuromatsu (Japanese black pine), Curved trunk, 150 years, 26 inches

Originating in the haven of dwarf trees, the Mikawa region near Nagoya, this bonsai has reached new levels of artistry with the touch of each succeeding owner. Like a dragon climbing to the heavens, the trunk of this tree rises from the earth with supreme strength.

### 22. Karin (Chinese quince), Triple trunk, 100 years, 27 inches

While each trunk seems to grow in its own quirky direction, together they form a unified, triangular shape. Devoted care has restored roundness to the branches and vitality to a once hollowed-out tree.

### 23. Ume-modoki (Holly), Triple trunk, 100 years, 26 inches

Open spaces between the clusters of berries reveal the contours of the trunks and branches. The two parent trunks overlook the smaller trunk to the right. *Ume-modoki* is often used in clump-style bonsai.

### 24. Goyomatsu (Japanese white pine), Curved trunk, 28 years, 24 inches

An awareness of angle and weight help maintain a calm secondary equilibrium between the main trunk and the dramatically protruding trunk. The lower branch was side grafted onto the main trunk, a process used to preserve rare and fine specimens.

The publisher gratefully acknowledges the following individuals and organizations who have kindly permitted the use of bonsai from their collections to be featured in this book:

Toshinori Suzuki
Kazuo Ohta
Seiichi Suzuki
Kihei Saito
Shin'ichi Nakajima
Hiroshi Takeyama
Takamasa Okano
Yukio Koide
Isao Shibata
Tohru Kaneko
Imperial Household Agency
Kohichi Nakayasu
Hideki Nakayasu
Jun'ichi Sato
Hiroshi Uehara
Takeshi Sugawara
Reiha no Hikari Kyokai

Enomoto Satsukien
Taro Enomoto
Hidekazu Ueda
Takarada Satsukien
Takeo Takarada
Kaoru Koizumi
Shiro Masuda
Tadao Yoshimoto
Yoshinori Ohta
Takayoshi Mori
Satoru Kusano
Ryohei Hirai
Naojiro Ando
Haruo Takagi
Masaru Ohshima
Myu Ad Center

NIPPON BONSAI ASSOCIATION

***Kuromatsu*** **(Japanese black pine), Cascade, 120 years, 45 inches**

Copyright © 1994 by Kodansha International Ltd. All rights reserved.

***Hime-mosochiku*** **(Bamboo), Natural, 5 years, 29 inches**

Copyright © 1994 by Kodansha International Ltd. All rights reserved.

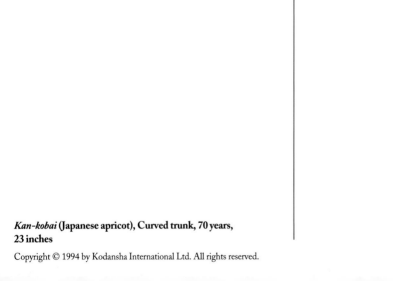

***Kan-kobai*** **(Japanese apricot), Curved trunk, 70 years, 23 inches**

Copyright © 1994 by Kodansha International Ltd. All rights reserved.

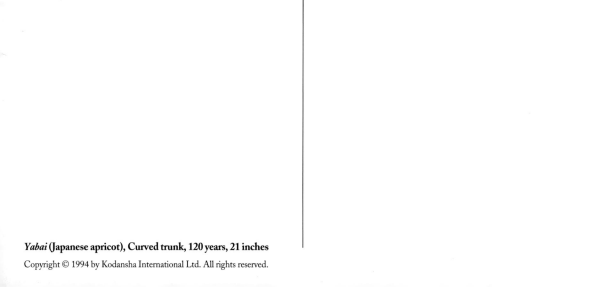

***Yabai*** **(Japanese apricot), Curved trunk, 120 years, 21 inches**

Copyright © 1994 by Kodansha International Ltd. All rights reserved.

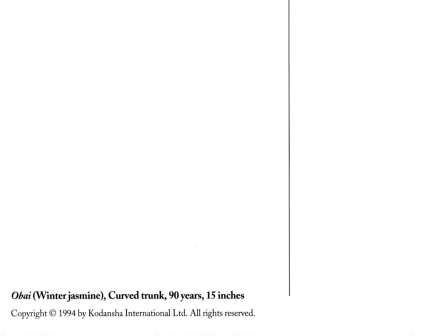

***Obai*** **(Winter jasmine), Curved trunk, 90 years, 15 inches**

Copyright © 1994 by Kodansha International Ltd. All rights reserved.

***Ume*** **(Japanese apricot), Curved trunk, 120 years, 26 inches**

Copyright © 1994 by Kodansha International Ltd. All rights reserved.

***Hinoki*** **(Japanese cypress), Straight trunk, 150 years, 45 inches**

Copyright © 1994 by Kodansha International Ltd. All rights reserved.

***Ezomatsu*** **(Yezo spruce), Root–linked, 200 years, 24 inches**

Copyright © 1994 by Kodansha International Ltd. All rights reserved.

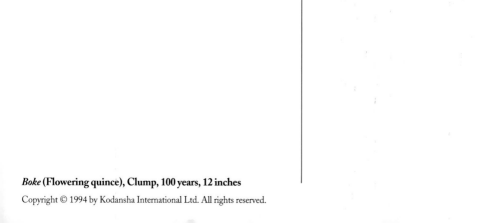

**Boke (Flowering quince), Clump, 100 years, 12 inches**

Copyright © 1994 by Kodansha International Ltd. All rights reserved.

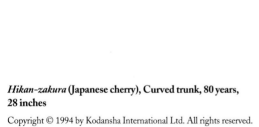

***Hikan-zakura*** **(Japanese cherry), Curved trunk, 80 years, 28 inches**

Copyright © 1994 by Kodansha International Ltd. All rights reserved.

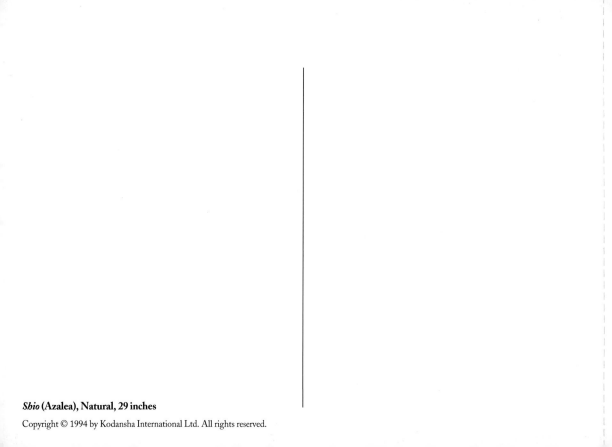

***Shio*** **(Azalea), Natural, 29 inches**

Copyright © 1994 by Kodansha International Ltd. All rights reserved.

***Takasago*** **(Azalea), Natural, 33 inches**

Copyright © 1994 by Kodansha International Ltd. All rights reserved.

***Yamatsutsuji*** **(Torch azalea), Clump, 100 years, 22 inches**

Copyright © 1994 by Kodansha International Ltd. All rights reserved.

***Kinsai* (Azalea), Natural, 23 inches**

Copyright © 1994 by Kodansha International Ltd. All rights reserved.

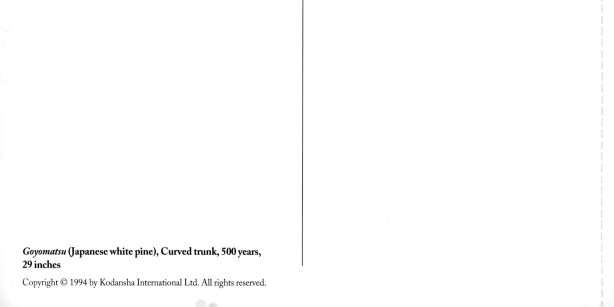

***Goyomatsu*** **(Japanese white pine), Curved trunk, 500 years, 29 inches**

Copyright © 1994 by Kodansha International Ltd. All rights reserved.

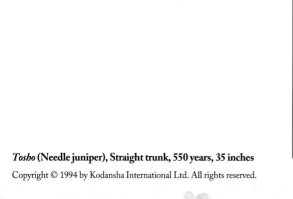

***Tosho*** **(Needle juniper), Straight trunk, 550 years, 35 inches**

Copyright © 1994 by Kodansha International Ltd. All rights reserved.

***Kaede*** **(Japanese maple), Twin trunk, 80 years, 34 inches**

Copyright © 1994 by Kodansha International Ltd. All rights reserved.

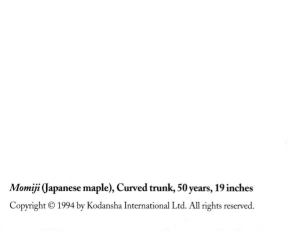

***Momiji* (Japanese maple), Curved trunk, 50 years, 19 inches**

Copyright © 1994 by Kodansha International Ltd. All rights reserved.

***Keyaki*** **(Japanese zelkova), Broom, 55 years, 28 inches**

Copyright © 1994 by Kodansha International Ltd. All rights reserved.

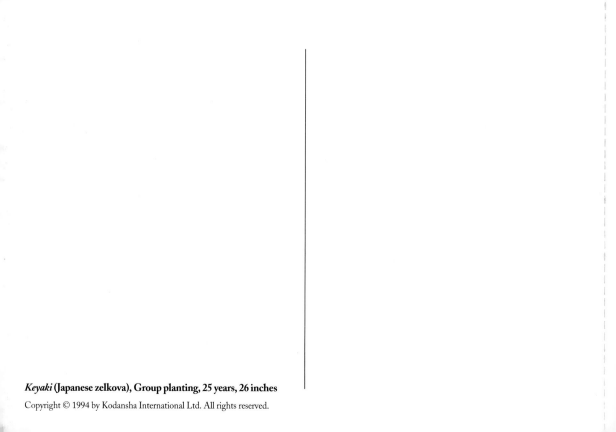

***Keyaki*** **(Japanese zelkova), Group planting, 25 years, 26 inches**

Copyright © 1994 by Kodansha International Ltd. All rights reserved.

***Kuromatsu*** **(Japanese black pine), Curved trunk, 150 years, 26 inches**

Copyright © 1994 by Kodansha International Ltd. All rights reserved.

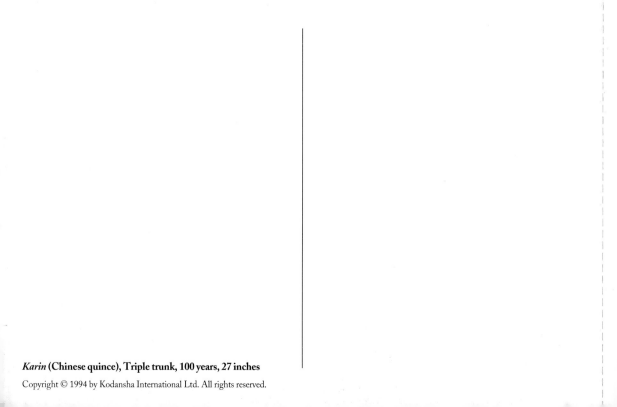

***Karin*** **(Chinese quince), Triple trunk, 100 years, 27 inches**

Copyright © 1994 by Kodansha International Ltd. All rights reserved.

***Ume-modoki*** **(Holly), Triple trunk, 100 years, 26 inches**

Copyright © 1994 by Kodansha International Ltd. All rights reserved.

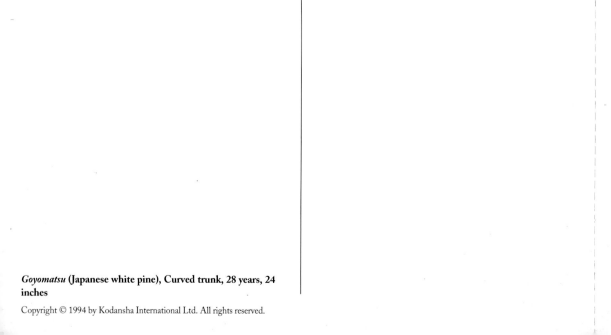

***Goyomatsu*** **(Japanese white pine), Curved trunk, 28 years, 24 inches**

Copyright © 1994 by Kodansha International Ltd. All rights reserved.